Animal World

S0-BTZ-691

Kangaroos

Christine Butterworth and Donna Bailey

RAINTREE STECK-VAUGHN
PUBLISHERS
The Steck-Vaughn Company

Austin, Texas

The sun comes up over
the grasslands of Australia.
The animals that live there
wake up and enjoy the warm sun.

The kangaroos let the warm sun
dry the morning dew on their fur.
Kangaroos feed on grass at night.
They sleep in the shade when
the day gets hot.

3

These are called red kangaroos.
They live together in
a group called a mob.

4

The biggest male in the mob
is called the boomer.
The boomer is as big as a tall man.
When he sits up, his tail
helps him balance.

He also uses his tail to balance
when he fights another male.
He grabs the other kangaroo with
his front legs and kicks him
with both back legs.

Female kangaroos are smaller
than the males.
Their fur is gray.
Can you see the baby kangaroo in
the mother's pouch?
Baby kangaroos are called joeys.

A joey lives in its mother's pouch
for nearly eight months.
The pouch is a pocket of skin on
the mother's tummy.

The mother gives the joey a bath
in the morning.
She licks the joey's fur to make it clean.
Then she licks her pouch to clean it, too.

9

This joey is eating grass beside its mother.
It pulls up the grass with
its long front teeth.
The kangaroos are too busy to see
the wild dog creeping up on them.

10

Australian wild dogs are called dingoes.
Dingoes are fierce hunters.
The boomer flicks his long ears.
He can hear the dingo creeping
through the grass.

11

The boomer thumps his back foot
to warn the mob.
The joeys jump head first
into their mothers' pouches.

The other kangaroos in the mob hop off
in all directions.
They take great hops with
their long back legs.

The joey has a fast ride
in its mother's pouch.
She jumps over a bush.
She can jump about seven feet
off the ground.

The boomer leans back on his tail and
gets ready to kick the dingo with
his back legs.
One kick can kill the dingo.
The dingo runs off into the trees.

The other kangaroos have jumped away.
When they are afraid, kangaroos
can hop 30 feet in one jump.
Some can travel almost 20 mph.

Now the mob has come together again.
There is no more danger from the dingo,
so the mob can eat and rest.
The kangaroos are tired.
They go to sleep in the shade of some trees.
This kangaroo is fast asleep on his back!

It is evening, and a male kangaroo
chooses a female from the mob.
The two kangaroos will mate
during the night.

After five weeks, the female
is ready to have her baby.
She leaves the mob to find
a quiet place under a tree.

The kangaroo licks her pouch clean.
She makes it ready for the new baby.
Her nipples are in her pouch.
The new baby will get milk from them.

20

The newborn kangaroo is tiny.
The baby looks like a little pink bean.
It is less than an inch long.
It has no eyes or ears.

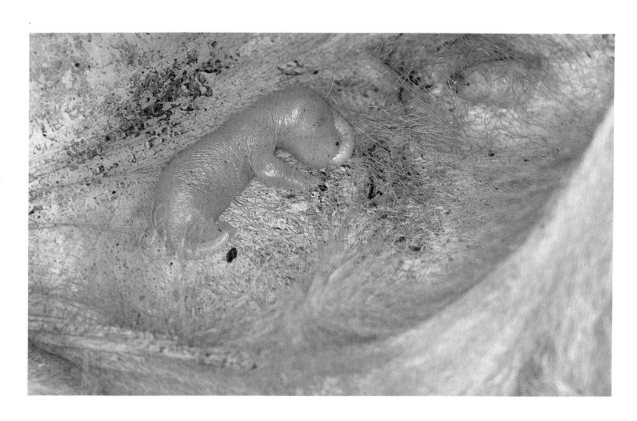

The tiny kangaroo has
little front arms and claws.
It pulls itself up the mother's fur
into her pouch.
The baby fastens its mouth
onto a nipple in the pouch.

The baby kangaroo, called a joey, stays inside
the mother's pouch and drinks her milk.
It grows a long tail, long ears, and
long back legs.
Joeys, like the one in the picture,
do not usually climb out of the pouch.

The joey is four months old now.
It lifts its head up and
looks out of the pouch.
It is much bigger and
has grown some fur.

The joey is now big enough
to leave the pouch.
It stays near its mother and puts it head
back in her pouch to drink the milk.

A bird calls, and the joey is scared.
It jumps back into the pouch.
Can you see the joey's tail as
it hides in its mother's pouch?

Now the joey is six months old.

It still drinks its mother's milk, but

it also begins to eat grass and leaves.

The joey stays close to its mother.
She warns the joey if an eagle or
a fox is nearby.
These animals like to eat joeys.

The mother will let the big joey
jump back into her pouch
when there is danger.
Then she carries the joey away
from the danger.

The joey is one year old.
It does not drink its mother's milk
any more.
She has another tiny kangaroo
in her pouch now.

The joey joins the rest of the mob.
The kangaroos keep a sharp lookout
for any enemies.

Joeys are grown up when they
are two years old.
They live with the mob.
Soon they will mate, and the females
will raise their own joeys.